371.8 Dubrovin, Vivian
DUB
        Running a school
        newspaper

$9.90

DATE			
Peterson APR 27			
JAN 18			

745

RUNNING A SCHOOL NEWSPAPER

RUNNING A SCHOOL NEWSPAPER

VIVIAN DUBROVIN

FRANKLIN WATTS

NEW YORK LONDON TORONTO SYDNEY

A FIRST BOOK

1 9 8 5

Library of Congress Cataloging in Publication Data

Dubrovin, Vivian.
Running a school newspaper.

(A First book)
Includes index.
Summary: Describes the features and options in a
student newspaper, the planning needed to organize
it, and the methods of producing it. Includes a style
sheet and glossary.
1. Student newspapers and periodicals—Juvenile
literature. [1. Newspapers. 2. Journalism] I. Title.
B3621.3.D83 1985   371.8'974   85-7476
ISBN 0-531-10046-4

88- 745 -11

CONTENTS

RUNNING A
SCHOOL
NEWSPAPER

INTRODUCTION

You want to publish your own newspaper. You want to report stories the way *you* see them. You want to express *your* opinion.

The people who founded our country believed it was so important for you to be able to do this that they made it—your right to publish your own ideas—a part of our United States Constitution. The First Amendment gives you freedom of speech. It guards your right to say or print what you want.

As with so many rights, however, freedom of speech is a two-sided coin. With the privilege goes responsibility. If you have the right to print what you want, you also have a responsibility to print the truth. Your readers expect the truth.

You probably can think of many things you are free to do as long as they don't hurt someone else. To print something that is not true and hurts someone, that is embarrassing, or damaging to that person's career is called *libel*. A person who is libeled can take the case to court and sue the newspaper.

If you tell the truth, try not to hurt anyone, and listen to the advice of your teachers and sponsors, you will be able to publish a fine newspaper.

What is truth? This is a classic question. Many people spend a lifetime seeking the answer.

If you sent three reporters to cover a story, you would get three different versions of the same event. Which one is true? They all are. Some people believe that the truth is found where the stories are the same, or where they overlap. This is one reason to read more than one version of any event.

In many countries newspapers are not free to report what they want. They can print only what the government wants to have published. This is called *censorship*. The government censors, or limits, what the newspaper can say.

Our First Amendment protects all our citizens from censorship.

Freedom of speech, truth, libel and *censorship* are very important words for every journalist. Learning to recognize them in everyday stories and events is one way to really understand what they mean.

Publishing your own newspaper is one of the best ways to learn how important newspapers really are, and to understand the role they play in our communities and our nation.

There is no one way to publish your newspaper. You have many choices. Your newspaper can be as simple or as elaborate as you want to make it. This book presents many of those choices, helps you plan and organize your paper, and shows you how to produce it.

Publishing a newspaper is an exciting adventure.

GETTING STARTED

Some of the most important hours you spend on your newspaper will be the hours you use to plan and design your new publication. The more planning you do in the beginning, the fewer problems you will have as you go along.

Before you begin to think of writing, you will need to make many decisions about what you want your paper to be.

PURPOSE

Why are you publishing a newspaper? What do you hope to accomplish? Think about these questions very carefully. All the rest of your decisions will depend on the answers you give for these questions.

What are some goals that your newspaper could have?

Report all school happenings
Help readers understand what goes on in the school
Express student opinion
Improve school image
Improve scholarship
Improve citizenship
Promote school projects
Broaden thinking of staff and readers

READERS

As you put your goals on paper, you will begin to get an idea of who your readers will be. Your readers might include:

Students
Teachers
Parents
School-board members
Community citizens

When you are able to think of who your readers are, you will begin to have an idea of what those readers want to know.

CONTENT

What will your newspaper include? Although you can always add to or discontinue certain parts of your newspaper, it's good to have a general plan for what your newspaper will include. Make a list of all the things you can think of that could be part of your newspaper. Then go over the list carefully and decide which things you would like in the first issue, which things you might add later, and which things you want to forget.

Here are some ideas you might want to consider:

News is something that has just happened or is about to happen. A news story can be written about any of the following:

School activity, such as a science or art fair
New equipment school has acquired
New programs offered
New teachers
Student government news
Faculty, student, alumni news
Educational news
Club news
Grade or classroom news, projects, speakers, etc.
New rules
Play to be presented
Awards/trophies earned
Library Week plans
Concerts at school
Parades
Ecology programs
Career programs
Achievement test days
Clean-up day
Recycling drives
Field trips

Features are those items that are not news stories. They can include interesting sidelights to news stories, columns, personality interviews, and sports articles. Some features you might consider are:

News-related features. (If you run a news story on the science fair, you might run a feature telling all about the winning exhibit. If a play is being presented, you could write a feature about the costumes or some of the actors.)
Lunch menus
New books in library
An opinion poll (how students feel about an event)
Puzzles/cartoons/short poems or sayings
Sports player of the week
Physical fitness program
Sports program (track or gymnastics)
Coaching staff
Field Day
"My Favorite Sport" (contributions or contest)

Columns are features, too, and might include:

Band or choir column
PTA column
Book, movie, or TV review
Fashions column
Crafts and/or models column
4-H or Scouts or other club activities
New boys and girls at school
Faculty member of the month
Food and cooking recipes
Honor roll (interview members)

Gardening column
Pet care column
Financial column (how to earn money, budget, save)
Years-ago column (how things were done at school twenty-five or fifty years ago)

Editorials

Written by newspaper staff
Guest editorials
The principal's column

Advertising

Classifieds
Display ads

STAFF

The more people you can get to help with the newspaper, the more interest you will create. Publishing a newspaper is a lot of work and you will welcome the extra hands, especially during the busy days.

The people who work on a newspaper are called the staff. Sometimes staff jobs are shared by more than one person. Sometimes one person has more than one job. While you are learning about newspaper production, it's a good idea to switch jobs now and then so that you can learn as many different things as possible and find out where your best talents are.

Here are some staff jobs you may want to consider for your school newspaper:

Publisher. The publisher is responsible for producing the newspaper. He or she decides who the editor will be and appoints other staff members. The publisher deals with the printer and is responsible for financial affairs. On a school newspaper the teacher or sponsor of the paper takes over the role of publisher.

Editor. The editor decides on everything that goes into the newspaper. He or she keeps track of school events, assigns stories, and assembles and checks material for each issue. The editor often writes much of the material, especially the editorials. The editor supervises the layout, and sometimes writes the headlines. *Co-editor.* The editor's job is so big that often two people share the responsibility. Co-editors have equal authority. *Assistant or associate editors* help the editor. They suggest story ideas, edit copy, write editorials, and help with layout, but they do not have the final say over what goes into the paper. An assistant editor's job is a good training position for next year's editor.

Reporters. The reporters write most of the news stories and features. Some reporters may concentrate on special assignments. Others compose regular columns. Reporters write something for each issue.

Contributors. Sometimes boys and girls who are not on the staff may contribute. Contributors usually do not write for each issue but submit material occasionally. Contributors might include other students, parents, teachers, or community members.

Copy Editor. The copy editor checks all copy for accuracy, grammar, and style. Sometimes the editor does this job. If someone on the staff is very good in English, that person would probably make a good copy editor and save the editor a lot of work.

Advertising Manager. If you plan to use many ads in your paper you will want an advertising manager and several advertising sales people. If you use only a few ads and your paper is not published very often, one person could probably do the job. The advertising people must have good public-relations skills and talk well with business people. *Advertising Production Manager.* On a newspaper the advertising production manager is not only responsible for getting the ads into camera-ready copy, but is also responsible for placement of the ads. (Ads go on the layout sheets before the news and features.) If there is not much advertising, one person can do both jobs. Someone must be responsible for checking the ad with the advertiser before publication.

Typographer. The typographer turns copy into type. He or she may either do the actual typesetting on a typewriter or word processor, or see that someone else gets the job done.

Layout Helpers. Layout people help paste up the dummy sheets. They proofread and do many little jobs that come up at the last moment. Helping with layout is a good way for new staff members to learn a lot about the newspaper.

Business or Office Manager. The business or office manager takes care of all noneditorial duties. He or she keeps the records, noting how much money is spent and what it is spent for. The records should include how many copies of the newspaper are sold. Someone good with math would be best suited for this job.

ORGANIZATION

Getting everyone to work well together is the secret of success on any newspaper. It is not easy to accomplish. You may need to try several methods and make changes to help each staff member do his or her best job.

A chart of "who does what" should be posted on the wall of the newsroom. This helps each person know his or her own job and whom to contact for other job information. Deadlines and beats can be included on this chart.

A calendar of events should also be posted on the newsroom wall. It should cover the entire school year and include everything that could be put into the newspaper. When news and features are suggested, you may need to consider which issue would be the best time to run the story. Deadlines for copy, typesetting, layout, and distribution for each issue should be entered in large red letters. The calendar must be continually updated.

Decide how often you will need to hold staff meetings and where. There are two important reasons for holding staff meetings. One is to plan the coming issue. Staff members can suggest news and feature ideas and the editor can assign work. The second reason is to evaluate the past issue. Evaluation means going over the entire issue, discussing the good and bad points, and deciding what changes should be made. In evaluating, remember that the negative points in each issue are as important as the successes. There is no way to improve your newspaper if you cannot recognize your weak points.

While you are thinking of what will be included in your newspaper and who will help do the jobs, you will also be thinking of how it will look when it is published. How big will the pages be? What kind of type and headlines will it have? How many columns of type will there be on a page?

Before you get too far with the design, talk to your printer. How will the newspaper be printed? Whatever method you use will have some limitations and you will need to work within those limitations. Will it be photocopied? This is the most popular method. But some newspapers are mimeographed or sent to a commercial printer.

Talk to your printer about size, type, headlines, columns, and photographs or illustrations. Do not be afraid to ask for an explanation of what you need to do. Almost every printer will have different requirements, and learning what those requirements are in the beginning will save a lot of time and problems later.

Be sure to investigate all possible methods in your school and community for printing your paper. While some methods may look cheaper, they may create so many problems that they are not really the best methods. Some methods are so much easier to use that they are worth a little extra cost. For example, photocopy pasteup is so much easier than typing stencils.

Some schools are setting up mini-publishing facilities in connection with their computer literacy programs. Word processing software and a printer can produce camera-ready copy for your newspaper. Adding a photocopy machine means that the entire publishing process can be completed at school.

After you have talked to your printer, you are ready to make decisions about the design. You may want to ask some art students to help you. Here are eight questions likely to come up:

1. Page size. How large will your page be? Will it be folded?

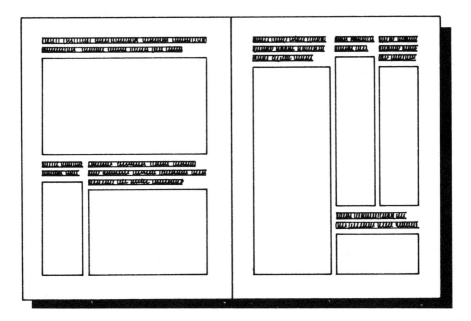

2. Column width. How many columns to a page? Will they all be the same or in a variety of widths?
3. Nameplate. The nameplate is the name of your newspaper as it appears on the front page.

The West Elementary Times

4. Front page folio line. Under the nameplate of each issue should be the day and date of that issue, volume number and issue number, place of publication, and price of a single copy. This folio line often has a rule above and below it.

Vol. 1, No. 6   5¢ West Elementary School, West, CO Tuesday, Dec. 10, 1985

5. Inside folio lines. Every inside page should have certain information across the top of the page: the name of the newspaper, place of publication, date, and page number.
6. Masthead. The masthead is the box on the editorial page that contains all the information about the newspaper. It should include:

    Name of the newspaper

    Folio information (date, volume, issue, and page number. This information is not across the top of the editorial page.)

    Place of publication and mailing address

How often the paper is published and on what day (for
   example, Wednesday for a weekly or first Wednesday
   for a monthly)
Copyright notice if copyrighted. (Many newspapers are not
   copyrighted.)
Name of publisher
Name of editor
Name and titles of other editors, reporters, advertising
   manager, and contributors for the issue
Single-issue price and subscription price (if any)
Advertising rates
Telephone number, office hours, and deadline dates

7. Column headings. Plan the special type that goes across the
   top of a regular column and is used in every issue.
8. Special section headings. Certain pages, such as the editorial
   page or sports page, may have headings of their own which are
   used in each issue.

DELIVERY AND SALES

How will you get your newspaper to your reader? Will it be free or
will it be sold? A newspaper that is sold for even a few pennies is
regarded more highly than one that is free.

How will you sell your newspaper? In the lunchroom or in the
classrooms or in the halls? Perhaps you can offer a subscription at a
special price.

Will you need to mail some copies to other schools, school
board members, or PTA officers? Perhaps your publisher will help
you make up a list of people who should receive a copy.

Who will deliver or sell the copies? Staff members or other
helpers?

STYLE SHEET

While you are planning, take time to create a style sheet. This is a set of rules, mostly grammar and punctuation, that everyone on the newspaper must follow. Since many people are writing and editing copy, there must be one set of rules.

Your English textbook can be a basic resource. There may be some rules you haven't learned yet, rules that you will need to use. The style sheet should have the rules you use most often in a handy, well-organized booklet or sheet. Each staff member should have a copy, and one should be easily available in the newsroom.

A sample style sheet is included on pages 61–71 of this book.

Unless you have a school directory or yearbook that includes the correct spelling of the name and position of every person on the school faculty, include this information in your style sheet.

You may add information to the style sheet at any time.

WRITING NEWS STORIES

A newspaper is not read from cover to cover the way a book is read. It has no table of contents or complete index to help you find stories.

A newspaper is designed in a special way to help you find the story you want to read. Because it is designed to be read in a certain way, it must be written that way.

Part of this special way is the headline. It tells in only a few words in big letters what the story is about. You should be able to decide from the headline whether or not you want to read the story. You could read just headlines in a newspaper if you wanted to do that.

If you read a newspaper news story, you should be able to find out all the important information in the first part. This first part is called the *lead*, and it may be in the first paragraph or in both the first and second paragraphs.

The lead should answer these questions:

who   what   where   when   why   how

For short, most reporters call this the five W's and H.

The rest of the story has more details in a descending order of importance. The least important information is last.

Newspaper readers can stop reading any place in the story. They can read just a few paragraphs or the whole story. They may be interested only in the main facts or they may want to read everything they can.

When the newspaper is pasted up, there may not be room for all of the story. The pasteup person may have to cut off the last paragraph or two. If the story is written with the most important news first, vital information will not be lost when the last paragraphs are cut off.

This special way of writing a newspaper story is called the *inverted pyramid*.

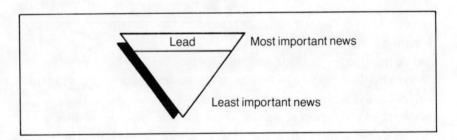

To write a news story:

1. Gather all the facts.
2. Make a list of the facts.
3. Find the five W's and H.
4. Using the five W's and H, write a lead.
5. Number remaining facts in descending order of importance.
6. Finish writing your story.

Here are some other hints to help make a good story:

1. Remember to use as many names as you can. People like to read their own names and other people's names.
2. Use as many *quotations* as you can.
3. Always try to tell who told you the information.
4. Use short, simple sentences that have a clear meaning.
5. Use as few words as you can to tell each idea.

FACTS AND OPINIONS

A news story should report facts. Tell only what happened or is going to happen.

It's tempting to tell what you think about what is happening, but that kind of opinion belongs on the editorial page, not in the middle of a news story. You might want to write an editorial about what you think. Talk to your editor and publisher about your ideas.

THE COMPLETE STORY

Some news stories continue to unfold through several issues of your newspaper. Sometimes all your friends know what happened before. But if someone just walked in the front door of your school, would that person understand the story? A good reporter makes sure her or his story is complete and not just an *update*, or the most recent news.

You may need to go back to a previous issue and copy parts of an old story. In this case, you write the new information first, then add the background information that explains the new information. Remember, unimportant facts and details come last.

For example, if a new computer finally arrives, you may want to tell of the year-long struggle to get it and all the cookie sales and aluminum can collections that made it possible. If a student wins a state competition, you may need to describe how she won the district competition several months before.

RECOGNIZING NEWS

Learning to recognize news in your school is just as hard as learning to write it. A good reporter learns how to take a *news tip* and turn it into an interesting story.

What is a news tip? A news tip is a *piece* of information.

Let's say you are covering a classroom beat. It's your job to check with all the third-grade teachers to see what's happening in their classrooms. One teacher tells you that his class is studying China. They have read some Chinese folk tales, made Chinese kites, and learned to draw some Chinese letters.

Now, some reporters would stop there. But a good reporter would talk to some of the boys and girls in class. What were some of the folk tales about? What kinds of kites did they make? The reporter would talk to some of the kite makers and find out why they made the kites they did, and if there were any problems. Did they try to fly them? A good reporter would tell what is special about Chinese letters. A good reporter might include a picture of a Chinese letter to print with the story to show how different Chinese writing is from our English.

When you receive a news tip, make a list of all the things that you would like to know. Then make a list of the people who can answer those questions. See how much information you can collect.

What additional information would you need and where would you go for the following news tips?

—if someone told you that there is a new boy in Ms. Smith's second-grade class. His name is Jimmy and he has a brother in sixth grade.

—if you learned that Mr. Collins's fifth-grade class is planning to put on a play and some parents are helping to make the costumes.

KEEP IT SHORT
AND SIMPLE

Writing a news story may sound difficult. It is not.

Keep your first stories simple. While you are learning how to write news stories, it is better to write three or four short news items about an event rather than one long one. More people will read the short ones.

Let's look at an example of how a short news story might develop.

During a staff meeting Dick discovers an interesting item on the school calendar. On April 25 and 26 there will be a spring art fair. April is still several months away, but Dick thinks his classmates should know about the fair so that they can get ready or have time to create something to exhibit. He raises his hand and volunteers to do a news story.

Where does he start?

He decides to poke his head into the school office to find out who is in charge of the spring art fair. The school secretary tells him that Ms. Carol Lyn, the art teacher, is handling all the arrangements.

Dick decides to interview Ms. Lyn. First, however, he tries to figure out what information he'll need to know. He makes a list of the five W's and H. Then he fills in the information he already has.

Who:
What: The spring art fair
Where:
Why:
When: April 25 and 26
How:

Dick decides to ask Ms. Lyn these questions:

1. Who can exhibit at the fair?
2. Where is it going to be held?
3. Why is there an art fair?
4. How do boys and girls enter? What should they do?

When Dick stops in Ms. Lyn's art room on the way back from lunch, he finds her sitting at her desk munching a sandwich and sipping a soft drink. She tells him to come in. She has a few free minutes to talk to him.

When he takes out his pad of paper and pencil and tells her why he has come, she gets very excited. This year's fair is going to be the biggest and best, she tells him. Why? Because she has changed the rules. This year anyone can enter the spring art fair. No matter where a student did the project—at school, at home, or in a club or organization—that project can be entered.

Ms. Lyn reaches toward a tall stack of papers, whips two from the top, and hands them to Dick. "I'm so glad you're doing a story for the newspaper," she says. "We want to get more boys and girls involved."

Ms. Lyn continues to talk. Many boys and girls, she says, create fine artwork on their own or in some club or organization. She pauses for a bite of her sandwich and Dick remembers his questions.

"Where will . . ." he begins.

"Becker Hall." She gulps the soft drink.

"How do kids . . ."

She waves her hand at the papers she gave him. . . . "Just fill in the entry form and bring it to me here in this room before April 20."

The bell rings and Dick knows he has to hurry to class. He thanks Ms. Lyn for her help and starts to leave. At the door he stops and fumbles with a question.

"Last year . . . ah . . . the rules you said are different. . . ." He knows he should look up last year's rules, but it's easier to ask.

"Last year only school projects created in class that semester could be shown. That really limited the exhibits that could be included. This year *anyone* can exhibit."

Dick runs down the hall to his class, slips into his seat and tries quickly to write down everything he can remember. What impresses him most is how excited Ms. Lyn was about the new rules and that this year everyone can exhibit. That'll be his main idea. The *who* in his story will be everyone.

Dick discovers that he forgot to ask, "Why?" Ms. Lyn did say she wanted to get more boys and girls involved, but is that really the "why" for his story? Should he go back and ask her again, or is this one of the ideas he is beginning to get for more stories?

Dick decides he has enough information for one simple news story. Maybe he could write an editorial about why an art fair is important.

He looks over the list of projects that could be exhibited. It's very, very long. Maybe he could do another story on what projects can be exhibited. Maybe he could do a feature on one or two of the projects. He'll do a story after the fair on what was exhibited and how many came and how successful it was.

Dick makes a list of all his ideas and puts it aside so he can concentrate on his first simple story about the spring art fair. Here is the story he wrote:

ART FAIR OPEN TO EVERYONE

Anyone can have an exhibit in the Spring Art Fair, to be held April 25 and 26 in Becker Hall. Just fill out an entry form in Ms. Carol Lyn's art room before April 20.

"We want to get more boys and girls involved," Ms. Lyn said.

Many students create some fine artwork on their own or in some club or organization, and Miss Lyn wants those projects to be shown at school.

For a list of the kinds of art needed, stop by Room 106 and pick up an idea sheet, or talk with Ms. Lyn after school.

Last year only school projects created in classes that semester could be entered. Ms. Lyn thought that was too limited.

Ms. Lyn hopes this year's Art Fair will be the biggest one Becker Valley Elementary School has ever had.

FEATURES

Features can be many things. Some people define a feature as anything in the newspaper that is not news or advertising.

One special thing about features is that they usually carry a *byline*. A byline is the name of the writer. A news story rarely has a byline.

An idea for a news feature can come from reading a news story. Brainstorming feature ideas in staff meetings is a good way to come up with many subjects.

WRITING FEATURES

A feature is not written in the inverted pyramid style you used for the news story. The lead for a feature story should catch the reader's eye, not just tell facts.

There are many ways to write a feature lead, but here are three to get you started:

1. A novelty lead arouses interest without telling everything.

MEET BECKY JUSTIN

If you enjoy showing horses you may have already met Becky Justin.

Becky moved to Westville from Somewherin, Ohio, just after school was out last spring.

She is active in 4-H and showed her horse at the County Fair this year. Becky and Pokey Boy won the beginning showmanship class in the Junior Horse Show.

Becky will be writing the 4-H News column for The Elementary Times.

Welcome to Westville, Becky!

2. A question lead asks a question.

NEW WORDS AND PICTURES SPELL HEALTH

Are tibia, femur, and pelvis part of a foreign language being taught in Mr. Jay Rentuso's fifth grade class? No! They are part of a new health program.

Last Tuesday Larry and Susan drew an outline of Jennifer on a large sheet of newsprint. On Wednesday Brenda, Todd, and Buzz drew in the tibia, femur, pelvis, and a lot more. On Thursday Lisa, Brad, and Harley labeled all the parts.

"It seems strange," said Jennifer, "to think that parts inside me have names."

"Not really," said Brad. "We all have the same *bones*."

3. A quotation lead starts with an interesting quotation.

STOCKING DOLL
WINS BLUE RIBBON

"I never thought my doll would win a blue," Julie Conners exclaimed when the judge pinned the first-place blue ribbon on her yarn-and-stocking craft project at the Spring Art Show, April 26.

Julie made the doll during a beginning dollmaking class at the YMCA. It was the first doll she ever made.

"I'm signed up for another class," Julie said. "I want to learn to make all kinds of dolls. It's fun!"

You should try not to cut off the last paragraph of a feature story because often it contains the punch line.

COLUMNS

"How will I ever find enough to write about to fill a monthly column for a whole year?" This worries some boys and girls, but columnists usually find the problem is the opposite: "How can I squeeze everything I want to write about into one little column?"

The secret is in the advance planning. At the beginning of the school year, make a calendar of all the events you might cover in your column. Note the publishing dates for the paper and your deadline for turning in your copy.

Let's say, for example, that you are writing a monthly column on the school band.

What things can you think of that the band does every year? When does it recruit new members? When are the concerts? Does it ever march in a parade or perform at a high-school band day? If so, put these happenings on your calendar and plan to do a column just before the event.

Are there scholarships to band camp? Did anyone go to band camp? You may want to interview those who went to camp, and use the information—either in the fall after camp or in the spring before the next camp.

Has the band gotten any new instruments or music? Does it own special instruments that it rents to students? Can you interview some of those students?

Sit down with the band director and find out about the year's program. Maybe you can do an article on the director.

Remember to include things that happen, such as an award the band or a member earns, a combo that forms and plays somewhere, or new rules for concert clothes.

Much of the material for your column may come from news events and interviews, but you may want to include minor, sometimes humorous, details, such as where to buy the black bow tie or white marching shoes, or that the band wears black socks and no shoes on concert night so they look alike and march quietly on stage.

If you write only one column a month, that's a total of nine columns during a school year. You may find yourself juggling to get everything in or shifting your April idea to February. And you may need to do some features or interviews in addition to your regular column.

Remember, the secret to the best columns is planning ahead, but don't be afraid to make changes to take advantage of unexpected happenings.

SPORTS

When your newspaper comes out only monthly, it is hard to report all the sports events. News, such as the score of a game, can be history before the newspaper is published. Most sports stories, therefore, turn into features. And, most sports stories tell about things that are going to happen, programs that are looking for members, or articles on boys and girls or teachers in special activities.

Here again, it's a good idea to plan in advance. You do not want ten sports stories in one issue and only one next time.

When does the gymnastic program begin? When do preparations start for Field Day? What are the rules for equipment during recess? Why? Schedule stories on your calendar.

Remember to research and add information to your sports stories just as you do with news stories. Whom can you interview? Where can you get background information?

Remember, also, that if you get information from books or magazines, you must retell it in your own words. You cannot copy other printed material word for word. That's someone else's story. You must create your own.

THE EDITORIAL PAGE

An editorial is the voice of the newspaper, the official opinion of the paper and its staff. It is through the editorials that a newspaper campaigns for improvements, changes, or action.

The editorials usually appear on their own page, the *editorial page*. The masthead appears on this page, and there is no advertising.

The editorial page always appears in the same place in every issue of the paper.

KINDS OF EDITORIALS

There are different kinds of editorials. Here are four that you might want to try to write.

Editorials that explain. Perhaps there is a current news story that calls for a lot of background information. Or there may be a need for understanding of a new program.

ALUMINUM CANS MAY PRODUCE CLASSROOM PUBLISHING

Will there ever be enough aluminum cans to buy a computer?

"Maybe not," said Marilou Coyne, president of Twin Rivers PTA, "but we want to try."

Mrs. Coyne told Journal editors that "the newspaper has done such a fine job of journalism that the PTA would like to help with some new equipment."

Many schools are creating classroom publishing facilities, she explained, by purchasing a computer and word-processing software and adding a printer and photocopier.

Miss Ellen Hines said her fifth grade could use this classroom publishing to produce books from a story writing project. Mr. Clyde Collins would publish a magazine of articles his sixth grade history class has written.

"Boys and girls want to see their words in print," Mrs. Coyne added. "There is no limit to the language arts projects that could be created."

The Journal staff would like to produce next year's newspaper on a word processor. Let's all collect cans for the Classroom Computer Publishing Program.

Editorials that criticize. These editorials should be constructive and not negative.

How do you think something should be improved? What should readers do to make things better?

GET BEST FIELD DAY TROPHIES

Are ribbons the most important thing at Field Day?

Some track and field players think so. They compete just to win, to get a ribbon.

Other boys and girls, however, treasure the friends they make on teams and the skills they learn in sports. These boys and girls realize that they are improving their health, their strength, and their understanding.

In every race there can be only one first place, a few ribbons. But everyone can be a winner if he or she knows what trophies to treasure.

On Field Day, let's count *all* our trophies. Let's not get so wrapped up in winning that we forget to have fun and enjoy the friends that are there with us.

Editorials that praise. When something has been very successful or somebody has done a very fine job, use some editorial space to give that "pat on the back."

THANKS FOR A GREAT FRAME-UP

Did you see all those tag board frames at the Art Show? Did you know they were all created by the same person?

Sara Romstein has stayed after school every day for two weeks to put all those exhibits in frames.

She carefully matched colors to add to the paintings, drawings, and prints. "I just took the same care I'd want someone else to use with my art," she said.

Thanks, Sara, for adding so much to our art show.

Editorials that persuade. These editorials are arguments and are also trying to change something.

MAKE FAIR PROJECT YOUR OWN

Many of the Science Fair projects last year were created with too much help from older brothers, sisters, and parents.

The projects were really great, and we all enjoyed them. But is the Science Fair held to attract spectacular exhibits, or to encourage boys and girls to create learning experiments?

It makes you feel good to have the biggest and best show in the auditorium. It's tempting to sit back and let others take over your production.

But what do you get out of it? If you want to learn new and exciting things, you have to do the work. The real fun is in the doing, especially when an idea you had is actually working.

Your parents' project may be fancier, but your own work is more rewarding.

This year let's accept advice and help from our families, but let's create the project ourselves so that we can experience the real rewards.

WRITING EDITORIALS

You usually take more time and put more effort into writing an editorial than you do for a news story. An editorial should be a finely polished piece of writing. In preparing an editorial, follow these steps:

1. Select a topic.
    The best ideas for editorials come from current school events or projects. Sit down with your teacher and other staff members and brainstorm all the ideas that are possible. Pick the

ones you like best. An editorial page can have more than one editorial.

2. Collect all the facts.
   a. Discuss with your teacher and staff what facts and background you may want to consider.
   b. Look up past articles in your newspaper, other newspapers, and books or magazines in the library.
   c. Interview people who can help.
3. Decide how to present your idea.
   A simple method of presentation is:
   a. A statement of the problem.
   b. The development of your case. Use facts, figures, quotations, information, or arguments.
   c. Summary statements that tell what you want your reader to do.
4. Make every word count.
   Your editorial should be brief and exact. Check it over again and again and cross out all words that are not needed. You can use "we" instead of "I" when writing editorials because you are talking about the editorial staff.
5. Write a snappy headline.
   The headline should catch the reader's eye and make him or her want to read your editorial.

LETTERS TO THE EDITOR

Letters your newspaper receives from readers can also appear on the editorial page.

Ask your classmates to contribute their ideas. Encourage them to be positive and constructive. The newspaper can edit or shorten the letters it prints.

Discuss all letters with your teacher/sponsor. Some letters will be very helpful, but some will not and may cause trouble for your paper. You do not have to print all the letters you receive.

Dear Editor,

I liked the article you had on "Clubs Anybody Can Join." I'm going to join the Model Rocket Club.

The school I came from didn't have a newspaper like yours. Sometimes notices about clubs were posted on bulletin boards. Sometimes they were announced over the intercom. Lots of kids didn't know about things they wanted to do.

Even my Mom and Dad read about the clubs. They liked the article, too.

Please keep writing about things to do and where to join.

Tim Mendalo

INTERVIEWING MEANS TALKING TO PEOPLE

For news stories, for features, and for many other articles, you will need to talk to people to get much of the information you need.

But not all of your information will come from talking to people. Some information will come from reading old articles, books, pamphlets, and notices. Any background material you can find on your subject should be gathered *before* your interview. It will help you prepare your questions.

Think carefully and plan before you begin looking for people to interview. What information do you need and who can help you?

You may need a lot of information from someone and only a word or two from someone else. When you need a lot of information, arrange a *formal interview*. When you need an item or two, an *informal interview* will be okay.

The *formal interview* is one that is carefully planned.

1.   Arrange a time and place for the interview.
2.   Tell the person what the interview will be about so that he or she can prepare for it in advance.
3.   Study your background material and plan your questions.
4.   Be on time and be polite.
5.   Let the person talk about other things if he or she wants to tell you something that is not in reply to one of your questions but relates to the subject.
6.   Forget some of your questions if they don't seem appropriate after you have talked for a while. You don't have to ask everything if you think you have all the information you need.
7.   Take a note pad with you and several pencils. Write down facts, numbers, dates, and names of persons and places. Take the time to be sure the spelling is correct.
8.   At the end of the interview, go over your notes with the person. Be sure you have understood correctly what he or she said.
9.   Write all the information down as soon as you can. You can organize it and write your story later, but get your information out of your head and onto paper as soon as possible.

Informal interviews are the passing remarks from classmates, on the way to school, in the hall, the lunchroom, or any other place where you might call out a question or they might offer information. Even though they are not planned, these interviews might become part of your story.

Carry a pad of paper in your pocket and remember to record the information when you receive it. If you are ever in doubt about what you remember, call the person and double-check. Don't guess.

DIRECT AND INDIRECT QUOTATIONS

The more quotations you use in your writing the more interesting and exciting it will be. If you can remember exactly what someone said, put quotation marks around it. This is called a *direct quote*.

"If the paper drive is successful," Ms. Jones said, "the winning class will have a party."

If you are not sure of the exact words, summarize what you think the speaker meant. This is called an *indirect quote*.

Ms. Jones said that there would be a party for the winning class in the paper drive.

Some TV programs show reporters being pushy and rude while trying to get a story. This is not a true picture of a good interview. On a school paper the news sources you work with are people you will need to talk to again and again throughout the school year. You will need to maintain a good relationship to get the best news. Remember your manners. Try to make all your news sources your friends and helpers.

HEADLINES
AND
CAPTIONS

Even though a headline comes first, ahead of the story, it is written last. Often it is not even written by the person who wrote the story. The copyreader, a person who checks the manuscript for accuracy, usually writes the headlines.

Why does one person write most of the headlines for the newspaper? Because writing headlines is a special job.

The headline is taken from the lead and summarizes the important facts in the story. It is a sentence, not a label.

To write a headline:

Choose the key words and the main idea of the story.
Use short words.
Cut out unnecessary words.
Use present and future tense.
Write a complete sentence with subject and verb.
Make the headline fit the space.

After you have written the headline you may have to divide it into two or three lines to fit the space.

You may want to hand-letter or stencil your headlines. Or, you may want to use transfer lettering. Transfer lettering comes in alphabet sheets and is available at office supply and art supply stores. Visit both stores and see what is available. Compare prices.

Whether you use transfer lettering or hand-letter or draw from stencils, you will need to count your letters to be sure your headline will fit. Count each letter, space, comma, etc. Never use a hyphen or split a word in a headline.

When you see a story with a headline, both seem to go together.

NEW STOP LIGHTS
AID SCHOOL CROSSING

New stop lights will soon make crossing the street at Fifth and Archer a lot easier.

"We've been trying to get these lights installed for three years," said PTA President Pat Andrews. "We're still working on Base Street and Fourth Avenue, and, of course, the highway overpass."

But, when you work with the story lead, you will see that many headlines can be written and all of them might be right. Which headline do you like best for this story? Could you write another one?

Fifteen Mountain View Junior High band members will give a concert and demonstrate their instruments to fourth graders at Becker Elementary School, Friday, May 2.

JUNIOR HIGH BAND GIVES CONCERT

FOURTH GRADERS
HEAR JUNIOR HIGH BAND

BAND MEMBERS
EXPLAIN INSTRUMENTS

FOURTH GRADERS
LEARN ABOUT BAND

CAPTIONS

Captions are the words under a picture or drawing that explain what it is about. They are written in complete sentences and must fit the space allowed.

Writing headlines and captions is a little like working puzzles. It can be a lot of fun once you get used to doing it.

PAGE
MAKEUP

Before you are ready to begin pasting your type onto dummy sheets, you have to decide what goes where.

THE FRONT PAGE

This part of your newspaper should be reserved for the most important news or news feature stories. Sort through your stories. Pick out the most important, the biggest news.

If you have something really big, you may want a banner headline, one that runs across all columns at the top of the front page. Use the biggest headline type that you have.

If you can't decide between two or three stories of equal importance, give them all headlines of the same size (but not a banner) and place them in positions of equal importance and pleasing appearance on the page.

Study the front page of your community newspaper for ideas.

The front page is not the place for editorials, the principal's message, the roving reporters column, or a group of funny pictures.

EDITORIAL PAGE

This page can have a special heading. It should carry your masthead (see page 12), editorials written by the staff, and/or the principal's message, and letters to the editor.

SPORTS PAGE

You may want to print all the sports stories on their own page with a special heading.

ENTERTAINMENT, CLUBS, AND ORGANIZATIONS

Other special columns can have their own pages, too, if you have enough material to fill a whole page.

You may want to run some specialty pages every other issue instead of trying to find enough material for each issue. Be careful that you do not let newsworthy items get too old.

FITTING AND FILLERS

When you wrote your news story, you knew that if the story was too long it might lose its last few paragraphs. But what happens when the story is too short and you are left with an inch or two of blank space?

You should keep a file of fillers. These are little tidbits of strange or unusual information, a tiny cartoon, or a drawing. It is anything that can be used to fill space. If you have been collecting fillers in an envelope or box, you can hunt for something the right size and shape whenever you need it.

Fillers are not timely and can be used in any issue. Be careful, though, that what you use goes with the other information on that page.

LAYOUT
AND
PASTEUP

Your stories have been written. Your headlines are ready. Everything has been set in type.

Now is the time to put it together. Now is the time to lay out and paste up the pages.

Some word processors allow you to position copy before you print it. If yours does, now is the time to arrange it.

Many typesetting methods require a pasteup. This means you take all stories and headlines and paste them onto a sheet of paper called a dummy sheet. You place and paste them just the way you want them to look in the paper. Your printer will photocopy your page.

It seems like a tremendous job. It is! But, there are some tricks that will make it easier.

Each page of the newspaper is pasted on a separate layout or dummy sheet. Even though your newspaper is printed back to back, or on both sides of the paper, each page is pasted up on its own sheet, one side only.

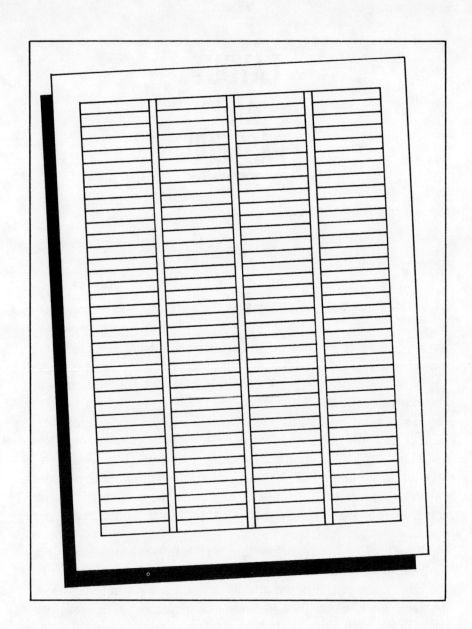

Prepare your dummy sheets well in advance, long before you are ready to lay out pages. Once you know page size and how wide the column will be, you can create the dummy sheets. On a sheet of paper the same size as your newspaper, draw an outline of the full type page and outline of columns. Draw horizontal lines every half inch. Have your printer run a supply of these in nonreproducible ink. You will use these to paste up your pages.

OTHER MATERIALS
YOU WILL NEED

Layout table. You will need a large table or several small ones set together where you can spread out many, if not all, of the dummy sheets for one issue.

Light table. This is a table with a glass top and a light under the glass. When you place a dummy sheet on the glass, the light shows your guidelines through the type, enabling you to position the type both horizontally and vertically. You can construct your own light table. It doesn't have to be fancy. But having a light source behind your dummy sheet can save time.

Rubber cement. To paste articles on layout sheets, use rubber cement. It allows you to pull pieces off and rearrange them if you change your mind. It does not wrinkle or curl paper as some glue will do.

Nonreproducible blue pens and pencils. At your office supply or art supply store, you can buy pens and pencils with light blue ink or lead that will not photocopy. You can use these to write or mark on your dummy sheets. You can write notes to the printer.

Scissors. You will need several for cutting type and headlines and fillers.

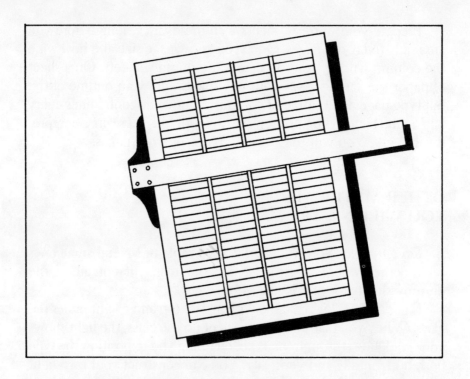

T square ruler. The T square is a ruler in the shape of a **T**. It is used to help line up copy so that it is straight on the dummy sheets.

White correction fluid. This is the white paint that typists use to correct mistakes. Use it to paint out anything that you do not want to print.

Transfer lettering for headlines or ads. Transfer lettering comes in many sizes and type styles and can be purchased at an office supply or art supply store. The letters are transferred onto paper by the pressure of your pencil. They are much easier to use than stencils and look more like real newspaper headlines. Visit your supply store to see what is available and check prices. You can use different size headlines in your newspaper, but do not choose too many different styles.

Stencils. You can use stencils to create headlines or you can hand-letter the big letters you need.

When your pasteups are finished, make as many photocopies of your newspaper as you will need.

ADVERTISING

It is not the subscription price, the amount the reader pays for the newspaper, that pays the bills. Advertising usually supports the newspaper.

A school newspaper may have some special funding to pay for its production. If it does, you may not need advertising. Yet, selling, designing, writing, and printing advertising in your newspaper is a learning experience that is worth far more than the effort involved. Advertising also increases the number of people interested in your newspaper.

What kind of advertising do you want to carry? There are basically two kinds for newspapers: classified and display ads.

CLASSIFIED ADS

Classified ads are small ads that appear in a special advertising section of the newspaper. They are called classifieds because they are grouped together by kind. There can be categories such as "Items for Sale," "Services," "Help Wanted," and "Wanted to Buy."

GIRL SCOUT UNIFORM, size 10, good condition. Call Betty Kwick, 777-5233.

FREE KITTENS, 8 weeks, orange tiger and calico. Call Sam, 311-4060.

The price of a classified ad usually depends on the number of words. You might charge twenty-five cents for fifteen words or a penny a word.

Advertisers usually write their own classifieds, or a staff person can help put together a brief ad.

Each classified ad should have a means of response, a telephone number, room number, or name and address. Even though your ad may run only a phone number, the newspaper business office should have a record of the advertiser's full name, address, and phone.

The newspaper staff might want to have a brainstorming session to list all the possible things for which classifieds could be used. The staff could then prepare a flyer to be circulated throughout the school, suggesting some of these uses.

"Sell your outgrown uniforms with a 10-cent ad."

"Homemade cookies by Karen."

Ads can come from students, parents, or business persons.

Check the classified sections of your local papers and other school papers. See how many ideas you can gather. Sell these ideas.

DISPLAY ADS

Display ads are the box ads that appear throughout the newspaper. They are placed on the dummy sheets before the news and features.

Call a staff meeting to get ideas of people who might want to advertise in your paper. Parents with businesses might want to place an ad, or stores near your school where students shop could also be interested.

RATES

Decide how much you are going to charge. Display ads are usually sold by the column inch. A column inch is 1 column wide and 1 inch deep. A display ad that is 2 columns wide and 3 inches deep is 6 column inches. Your charge for this ad would be your unit cost (price of printing a column inch) times six.

Determine how much it costs to print your newspaper. How much per page? How many columns are there per page? How many column inches are there on a page? Your display ads should sell for more than it costs you to print them if you want your ads to pay the printing costs of your entire newspaper. But do not make them so high that nobody will buy them.

SAMPLES

Design a few sample ads to show customers what an ad in your newspaper could look like. Create small and large square and rectangular ads. Show how large and small type and drawings might look.

SELLING THE AD

Take your sample ads and ad rates and talk to your customer. Find out what the customer's needs are, and try to create an ad that will fill those needs. Is she or he selling a product or a service?

SET AD IN TYPE

Write the copy or use the copy the advertiser has submitted. Set the copy in type. Hand-letter or use transfer type for the large type.

PROOFREADING AND
FINAL APPROVAL

Check the ad over very carefully. Be sure it says what the advertiser wanted it to say and that there are no errors.

Show the advertiser a copy of the ad the way you plan to run it in your newspaper. Be sure she or he okays it. It is a good idea to get this okay in writing. Have the advertiser initial a sample copy.

PLACEMENT ON
THE DUMMY SHEET

Paste the ad on the dummy sheet where you want it to appear in the newspaper. News stories and features are placed around the ads.

BILLING THE ADVERTISER

Be sure your advertiser sees a copy or several copies of the newspaper that contains the ad. Try to collect payment either when you sell the ad or deliver the newspaper copies.

Happy advertisers buy more ads and recommend your newspaper to other people. Try to keep your advertisers happy.

FUTURE ISSUES

After you finish the first issue of your newspaper and it has been distributed to your readers, what do you do? Do you take a short rest before you start on the next one?

Newspapers and magazines are not printed one after another even though you see them appear that way on the newstands. At any given time a newspaper or magazine will have at least three issues in production.

One issue (the current one) will be in the printing and distribution stage. The next issue will be going through the layout and the typesetting process. The third issue will be in the writing and editing stage.

Let's say that you are distributing the September issue of your monthly newspaper. Your October issue should be getting set in type and almost ready for layout and pasteup. Your November issue is being written and edited.

Your September staff meetings, then, may consist of assigning stories for the November issue.

This may seem very confusing, but it really is not. This is where your planning ahead, your charts on the wall, and your calendar with events and deadlines become so important. When everyone on your staff knows what has to be done, your newspaper will be a smoothly running operation.

Deadlines are very important to this smooth process. Everyone must meet his deadline so that the next person can do his job.

Your publication date is also very important. If May 8 is on your folio line, then May 8 is the day your newspaper is first distributed. If your masthead says the first Wednesday in the month, even though your folio says only May, your newspaper must be available that first Wednesday in May. Your newspaper can be sold every day for the rest of the month, if you have enough copies, but it must be available on that first day, the publication date.

If you have ever had a newspaper delivery route, you know how readers feel about receiving their papers when they expect them. Your readers want your newspaper on time, too.

Your local newspaper can be a good source of ideas. Other school newspapers can also help. The more you read, the more fun your newspaper adventure will become because new ideas put the excitement into publishing.

You may want to put a bulletin board on your newsroom wall. This may be the place to post ideas for the staff to think about. It may include items you clip from other papers. You might want to tack up articles from other papers about events at your school or articles that show how other school papers handled events at their school.

Sharing ideas is part of the fun. Publishing a newspaper is most exciting when it is a team project.

SAMPLE STYLE SHEET

A style sheet contains rules for the writing in your newspaper. Just as athletes must all follow the same rules for a game, reporters and other contributors must also follow the same writing rules for a publication. You might want to use this style sheet and add to it, or create your own.

SPECIAL TREATMENT OF WORDS

Using Names
Use *Mr., Mrs., Miss, Ms.,* or other proper titles with the names of teachers and other adults.

 Dr. Joan Martinez
 Coach Ben Johnson
 Mr. Henry B. Higgens

The first time you use a person's name in a story, use the full name. Never use only one initial. Be sure all names are spelled correctly.

Mrs. B. L. Hill
Jamie Lincoln

The first time you use a person's name in a story, identify the person with his or her proper title. The title usually follows the name but can come first. Do not capitalize the title unless it is used instead of Mr., Miss or Ms.

Mr. M. A. Jones, superintendent of schools
Sam Winston, secretary
Principal J. J. Lasero

After you have used the name once, use Mr., Mrs., Miss, or Ms. with the last name for adults. Use the first name for a student.

Mrs. Hill
Jamie

This is a good place to list every person on the faculty and staff of your school. Spell names correctly and give proper titles.

Using Capital Letters
Use capital letters for all proper nouns.
    This includes months, days of week and holidays.

May
Monday
Christmas

The style sheet also includes the names of schools, clubs, organizations, cities, streets, and geographical areas.

Cedartown Elementary School
Chicago
Seventh Street
Girl Scouts
the Southwest

It includes the names of races and nationalities.

American
Negro
Oriental
(use small letters for black, white, etc.)

It includes nicknames of teams.

Cowboys
Tigers

Use capital letters for one-word titles when they come before the name.

Superintendent Gary Landen
Director H. B. Hoffmann

Use capital letters for the main words in the title of a book, play, movie, or song. Capitalize any word that comes first in the title.

The Mystery of the Three Swans
A Midnight Adventure

Using Lowercase Letters
Use small (lowercase) letters for school subjects, except languages and course names.

> *history*
> *French*
> *math*
> *Spanish*
> *journalism*
> *Journalism 101*

Use lowercase letters for words like *club, street, band* when they are used alone without a proper noun.

> *The Math Club met yesterday.*
> *The band will play in the parade.*

Use lowercase letters for titles used without a proper noun.

> *The principal opened the door.*

Use lowercase letters for:

> Seasons of the year, such as *summer, winter.*
> Names of classes, such as *sixth grade, junior in high school.*
> Time of day, such as *a.m.* and *p.m.*
> School rooms, such as *cafeteria, room 102, boys' gym,* unless it is used with a proper noun, such as *Tyler Auditorium.*

Abbreviations
You can abbreviate long names of organizations or other familiar names.

Use no spaces or periods between letters.

PTA, YMCA, TV

Do not abbreviate or use signs for percent, distances, weights, or degrees. Write it this way:

40 percent, 95 degrees, 8 pounds, 4 feet 8 inches, 1 liter

Dates And Times
Write dates one way, *September 9.* (Never write *January 4th or 7 October, or the 12th of July.*)
Do not use *on* before days or dates.

They met Thursday.
They will march April 5.

Do not use the current year, coming year, or past year.

November 11
last August
next January

Do not use *o'clock* or zeros for even hours. Write it this way:

4:15 p.m.
9 a.m.
12 noon

Numbers
Spell out numbers one to nine and use figures for numbers 10 and above.

Exceptions:

In a sentence that contains some numbers below 10 and some above 10, use figures for all.

Always use figures for ages, sizes, money, percents, degrees, days of the months, hours of the day, scores, room numbers, page and chapter numbers, and street numbers.

> *10 years old*
> *5 dollars*
> *4 feet*
> *25 cents*
> *100 percent*
> *chapter 4*

Use *st, nd, rd* or *th* with numbered streets over Ninth, but not with dates.

> *North 22nd Street*
> *East 16th Street*
> *November 21*

If money is under $1, use numbers and the word *cents*. For $1 or more, use the dollar sign. Do not use zeros when they are not needed.

> *45 cents*
> *$7*
> *$2.50*

Do not begin a sentence with a figure. Spell it out or rewrite the sentence.

PUNCTUATION

Using Commas
Use a comma to separate words in a series.

There were yellow, green, and blue balloons.

Use commas around identifications.

Tom Barton, chief of police, spoke to the third grade.

Use commas to set off quotations.

"I called you," Jimmy said, "to invite you to my party."

Use commas in addresses.

Mrs. Carol Benito, 2691 Carter Street, Weston, Arizona

Use commas in numbers over 999 except in street numbers or telephone numbers.

9,487
303-776-5432
6472 Alton Way

Use commas in scores of sports games.

Westville 15, Tompson Valley 7.

Use a comma before *and*, *but*, and *or* in a compound sentence.

Using Semicolons
Use a semicolon between main divisions of a listing.

> The new officers are Betty Haley, president; George Ott, vice-president; Judy Johnson, secretary; and Mark Kale, treasurer.

Using Colons
Use a colon to introduce a series or a list.

> The following students received awards: Barb Ryan, Trudy Myers, Antonio Mendez, Joe Lindell, and Andrew Cole, Jr.

Use a colon to separate minutes from seconds in sport times.

> Joe's time was 4:15 (four minutes and 15 seconds)

Using an Apostrophe
Use an apostrophe to form a possessive.
  If the word is singular, add an apostrophe and s.

> Tom's book
> the book's first page

If the word is plural but does not end in s, add an apostrophe and s.

> Children's books and men's hats are two items.

If the word is plural and ends in s, add only an apostrophe.

> Girls' team sports will begin Monday.

Use an apostrophe in contractions or to show that a letter or number is missing.

don't use '84

Use an apostrophe to form plurals of letters and figures.

too many Q's, but not enough 8's

Using Quotation Marks
Use quotation marks to show the exact words of a speaker.
An indirect quotation does not need quotation marks.

"There will be a party for the winning room," said Ms. Collins.
Ms. Collins said the winning room would have a party.

If a quotation includes several paragraphs, use quotation marks at the beginning of each paragraph and at the end of the last one.

For a quotation within a quotation use single quotation marks.
Periods and commas are always put inside the quotation marks.
Question marks and exclamations are inside the quotation marks only if they are part of the quotation.

Did you read "The Adventures of Superdog"?
"Are you finished now?" he asked.

Start a new paragraph each time there is a new speaker.

Using a Hyphen
Use a hyphen between syllables to divide words at the end of a line.

Use a hyphen in compound words.

> *vice-president*
> *all-state*
> *50-yard line*
> *three-day trip*

Use a hyphen in sports scores.

> *Ridgeview won 9-3.*

Using a Dash
Use a dash in calendars or columns.

> *March 22—Volleyball, Eastvale, here.*

Do not use a dash instead of periods, commas, colons, or semi-colons in sentences.

WRITING TITLES

Use quotation marks for titles of plays, poems, chapters, movies, TV programs, and songs.

> *Underline book titles.*

Capitalize newspaper and magazine names but do not underline or put quotation marks around them.

SPELLING

Any dictionary can be used to check spelling and how to hyphenate words. But once you have selected the dictionary you want to use, stick with it. Because dictionaries sometimes differ in their treatment of words (whether a word is hyphenated, set as two words, or set as one), for the sake of consistency you should always use the same dictionary.

GLOSSARY

Banner: a headline across the entire page.

Beat: a news source that a reporter visits regularly.

Body: all of a news story after the lead.

Body type: type used for all material other than ads or head-lines.

Boldface: printed letters in darker type. **This is boldface**.

Box: lines around printed type or around display ad.

Byline: the author's name, usually printed in small type below the headline. "By Joe Smith"

Camera-ready: copy and art ready to be photographed for repro-duction without further changes.

Captions: words below a picture which describe the illustra-tion.

Circulation: the process of distributing a newspaper to its readers; also, the total number of copies distributed each issue or year.

Classified: small ads that are arranged or "classified" by category.

Column: an article written regularly by the same person, expressing his or her opinion; also, the vertical row of type on a page. There may be two or three such columns.

Columnist: a person who writes a column that appears in a newspaper.

Contributor: a person who is not a member of the staff but who contributes material, usually on an irregular basis.

Copy: written material before it is put into type.

Copy editor: person in charge of copyreading. May do the job or supervise copyreaders.

Copyreader: person who checks copy for errors; also, usually writes the headlines.

Copyright: the author's right to control the publication of his or her work. Material that is copyrighted may not be reproduced without the consent of the copyright holder.

Copywriter: a person who writes copy.

Cover a story: get all the facts about an event.

Deadline: date that material is due.

Display ad: advertisement with large display type, usually within a box.

Display type: large type used in headlines and ads.

Dummy sheets: the pages on which the stories, headlines, and ads are pasted. Looks just like the final page will look. Your newspaper can be photocopied from the dummy sheets.

Editor: person responsible for the content of all or certain parts of the newspaper. *Co-editors* have equal authority. *Assistant* or *associate editors* help the editor but do not have final say over what goes into the paper.

Editorial: an article that gives the official opinion of the newspaper and its staff. It is usually written by the editor and appears on its own page, the editorial page.

Features: anything in a newspaper that is not news or advertising. Can include articles, columns, interviews, book reviews, etc.

Five W's and H: information that should be in the lead of an inverted pyramid story. It stands for *who, what, where, when, why, and how.*

Fillers: short pieces of information used to fill space in a column or page.

First Amendment: the First Amendment to the Constitution of the United States guarantees free speech. This gives newspapers the right to print what they want without censorship.

Folio line: a line of type on each page of the newspaper. The *front folio line* usually runs under the nameplate and includes the day and date of the issue, volume and issue numbers, place of publication, and price of a single copy. *Inside folio lines* appear on every inside page (except the editorial page) and contain the name of the newspaper, place of publication, date, and page number.

Galley proof: a long sheet of copy set in type, usually one column wide, that is used to check for errors. The type on the galley can be used to cut and paste up the pages on the dummy sheets.

Headline: large type above a story which summarizes the story. A headline is not a title or a label. It is a sentence. Sometimes some of the words are implied, but it should make a statement.

Italics: a slanted type. *This is italics.*

Journalist: person who collects, writes, and edits news.

Layout: the plan or arrangement of stories, features, and ads on the page.

Lead: (pronounced *leed*) the first paragraph or two, summarizing the entire news story. It should contain the five W's and H.

Libel: written material that hurts someone; something that is embarrassing or damaging to his or her career.

Masthead: a box of information about the newspaper. It usually appears on the editorial page. (See page 12.)

Nameplate: the type that gives the name of the newspaper.

News: information about something that has just happened or is about to happen.

Novelty lead: a lead for a feature story that arouses interest and does not tell everything.

Page makeup: the arrangement of all material on the page according to layout. The pasteup of copy, headlines, and advertisements on the dummy as they will appear on the final page.

Photocopy: make a photographic reproduction of copy.

Proofread: to check galley proofs for errors.

Proofreaders' marks: symbols that a proofreader uses to show what corrections should be made in type.

Publisher: the person who is responsible for seeing that the newspaper gets published. On a school newspaper the publisher may be a teacher/sponsor.

Question lead: a feature story lead that begins with a question.

Quotation: something that someone says. A *direct quotation* is the exact words that someone used; it is placed between quotation marks. An *indirect quote* is a summary of what was said and is not placed in quotation marks.

Quotation lead: a feature story lead that begins with a quotation.

Reporter: a person who gathers news and writes the news stories. A reporter usually writes for every issue of the newspaper.

Staff: all of the people who work on the newspaper.

Stet: proofreader's mark meaning leave as it was.

Style sheet: the rules of writing used on the newspaper. Most newspapers have their own style. All reporters and contributors must follow the same style.

Summary lead: a beginning paragraph of a feature story that summarizes the article.

Type: letters used in printing.

Typographer: person who sets copy into type.

Update: the most recent news in a continuing story.

PROOFREADERS' MARKS

⁋   paragraph

NO ⁋   no paragraph

(CO)   (4)   spell out

(fifteen)   change to figure

∧   insert

℮   take it out

℮   take out and close up space

(stet)   leave as it was

in between. ⌐ The next day	run in
#	add aspace
(tr)	transpose words
(tr)	transpose letters
(cap)	change to capital letter
(lc)	Change to lowercase letter
⌐ ⌐	indent both sides, center material in column
⊙	notice period (so typesetter won't miss it)
⌃,	notice comma
⌃;	notice semicolon
⊙:	notice colon
(bf)	set in boldface
(ital)	set in italics
(S.C.)	set in small caps
(30)	end of story

INDEX

ABOUT
THE AUTHOR

Vivian Dubrovin has been writing for as long as she can remember. When in elementary school she wrote plays and pageants that her classmates performed on the school stage. In high school she worked on the school yearbook and newspaper. She graduated from college with a degree in journalism.

While raising two boys and three girls she became interested in children's literature. Her recent achievements include stories for multi-media educational reading programs, and stories and articles for children's magazines. She has also directed regional workshops on writing for children and has served as a consultant for many school and individual writing projects.

Her book *Write Your Own Story*, published by Franklin Watts in 1984, has become the basis for her Story Writing Workshops in elementary classrooms and her teacher seminar programs on writing.